UNITY®

100 YEARS
OF
FAITH & VISION

Unity Books
Unity Village, MO 64065

Acknowledgments

Unity School of Christianity gratefully
acknowledges the following for their literary,
editorial, and artistic contributions to this book:

Robert R. Barth, Margaret F. Dale, William B. Dale,
Charles R. Fillmore, Connie Fillmore, James Dillet Freeman,
Sue Jackson, Tony La Tona, Foster McClellan, Keith McKinney,
Wayne Manning, Harry Morgan, Glenn Mosley, Jim Rosemergy,
John A. V. Strickland, James K. Walker, Katherine Weedman,
and Pamela Yearsley.

The light that shines for you

Prologue

Unity Tract Society, 1315 McGee Street, Kansas City, Missouri (circa 1898)

Charles R. Fillmore
Chairman of the Board of Trustees
Unity School of Christianity

Our spiritual movement began when my grandparents, Charles and Myrtle Fillmore, were inspired to launch the publication of *Modern Thought*. This journal of metaphysical philosophy was ahead of its time and, from a humble beginning in mid-America, evolved into a school of Christian ideas that has had worldwide influence.

Scientists speculate that the universe began about fifteen billion years ago and that our earth has existed for at least four and a half billion years. Compared to such a mind-stretching concept, 100 years seem less than a microsecond. However, when we consider the changes made in all areas of human experience during this time, the last century becomes the most important in all history. We in Unity believe that our founders and their followers have made important contributions to humankind's search for spiritual understanding through this exciting time of human advancement.

Beginning eclectic in their religious approach, the Fillmores soon concentrated their efforts on seeking practical methods for applying Christianity to daily living. As they studied and meditated on the teachings of Jesus Christ, they came to believe firmly that Jesus is infinitely more than a Deity, and that to worship Him only as the Son of the Almighty is to miss the main points of His life and teaching. Thus, Unity concentrated on seeking to understand the divine principles for successful living underlying the literal word of *The Gospels*. This "metaphysical interpretation of Scripture," as they called it, was applied to the Old Testament as well as the New and gave rise to mind-stretching insights.

Early in the twentieth century, revelation also led the Fillmores to select the name *Unity* for their work. This decision was fortunate, for it describes the movement's basic belief better than any other name; this belief being that we are all children of one Creator and are spiritually united with God and with all other people everywhere. This does not mean that we must be the same in belief, thought, and expression, for there is unity in diversity.

Also, the word *movement* is apt in describing our first 100 years. It denotes growth and expansion rather than the preservation of the status quo and the resulting stagnation. We believe that a religious system should be open and flexible with the ability to accept new revelations of our relationship to God as they are progressively disclosed. Thus, Unity emphasizes that, consciously or not, we all seek better understanding of God's limitless intelligence. Our leaders are students as well as teachers since no one has

Myrtle (Page) Fillmore (circa 1863)

Early prayer group (circa 1890)

Charles Fillmore (circa 1876)

complete knowledge of Truth. We are all fellow members in life's fascinating classroom.

What has Unity accomplished in the past century? Its influence has reached far beyond those who consider Unity to be their only religious affiliation. Unity ideas concerning spiritual healing, positive thinking, brotherly love, freedom from undeserved feelings of guilt, and the justification of personal prosperity are widely understood to be desirable characteristics of a full life. These and many other concepts pioneered by Unity have been accepted by thinking people the world over.

"We are all fellow members in life's fascinating classroom."

Silent Unity Healing Room, Ninth and Tracy, Kansas City, Missouri (circa 1943)

Perhaps Unity's most important contribution to today's religious thought is our approach to prayer. Rather than the beseeching supplication of tradition, Unity advocates prayer as a method of attunement to divine wisdom through proper preparation and receptivity. We don't pray to change God to do our will but to make ourselves open to recognizing, understanding, and accepting God's will. We as individuals can be helped in our faith and ability to receive answers to prayer by joining others of like mind. Thus, the prayer ministry of Silent Unity has been praying with and for all who ask for help for most of the last 100 years.

How has Unity's message of faith in God's plan of good for His creation been spread? The first Unity "missionaries" were publications, books, and booklets, and they continue to provide an important outreach. Next, personal contact in the form of trained Unity leadership has seen steady growth as shown in the increasing numbers of Unity centers and churches in the United States and overseas. Unity School has added radio, television, audiocassettes, and videocassettes to its ministries.

Conducted at Unity headquarters, refined and varied in-residence educational programs designed for personal spiritual growth as well as qualification for Unity leadership are re-emphasizing "school" in Unity School of Christianity's name. We believe that the aforementioned ministries have had a positive influence beyond the boundaries of the Unity organization. Acceptance of Unity ideas by any and all receptive minds and hearts is certainly in keeping with our founders' purpose and desire.

As I review my own lifetime involvement in Unity, vivid memories of Unity people flood my mind. A remarkable number of inspired and inspiring folks from all of life's stations have been attracted by the philosophy and the desire to help spread it. My childhood memories are of interesting individuals from near and far who came

Unity Farm produced abundant crops of fruits and vegetables.

to Unity headquarters attracted by my grandparents' work. Most came to learn, others to discuss, some to argue, and many to serve. One was a man of simple tastes and deep intellect, who arrived at a time when a gardener was needed. He readily accepted the humble position and salary that went with it, was content to dwell in Unity Farm's spartan boarding-house, and faithfully and skillfully looked after the flowers and vegetables. With equal loving care he tended the budding minds of his Unity Farm Sunday School students as our teacher, counselor, and consoler. His given name was the same as a Texas city, and his family name was that of an Indian tribe, and for many years he was a blessing to all he contacted.

Unity Farm cabins in the early stages of grounds development

Another who made a strong impression was the scion of a wealthy eastern family, who came to Unity seeking freedom from an alcohol challenge. Good-humored, well-educated, and of stately bearing, he soon became the official greeter and tour guide for Unity School. He excelled in several sports and helped lay out the first golf course and tennis courts at Unity Farm. I was fascinated by his seemingly effortless ability to whip local athletes half his age on the courts and fairways. I believe that he found peace and renewal at Unity.

As mentioned, in the early days of the Unity Farm before it became Unity Village, there was a need for farm workers and a place for them to live. The answer was a boardinghouse for the single men. Their living quarters were in a long building with bunk rooms, and meals were served in a connecting dining room by the most energetic lady I have ever known. She provided three meals a day for a crew of a dozen men as well as taking care of her own four-member family. Also, she tended a large chicken house and operated the Farm's telephone switchboard. Later she kept house for male student ministers and played an important role as their unofficial housemother. Needless to say, she was a pearl without price, and her services were invaluable.

"The Swimming Hole," Unity Farm (early 1900s)

From time to time Unity attracted outstanding Truth teachers. One was a distinguished man, who had a divinity doctorate from a major Protestant denomination. He came to study with Charles Fillmore, became ordained in Unity, and was persuaded to stay on to teach. He brilliantly reorganized the training school for prospective teachers and emphasized study of the New Testament. His own classes were most popular and his lessons on the Apostles so vivid that a student once remarked, "Doctor, when you teach Paul, we can see him coming down the aisle!"

Men of Unity Retreat (circa 1961)

When Unity retreats began in the Village, October was the month for a "men only" event. I was in charge of the program and scheduled a sharing session for all who wanted to participate. Most told of Unity's influence in their lives and, though inspiring, had a tendency to become repetitious. One fellow, a shy man of small stature, hung back.

When pressed to share with the group, he said, "Well, I love Unity, but all I can do is sing 'Ole Man River!' " Accompanying himself on the piano, he held us spellbound with his rendition of Jerome Kern's classic. His *basso profundo* rattled the doors of the chapel, and when he finished, we were dumbstruck by the magnificence of his voice. Finally the ovation broke forth, and he was given an accolade that was barely short of carrying him around the room on our shoulders. Thenceforth he was asked to perform at every opportunity, and his singing was the highlight of Men's Retreats for several years.

I have fond early memories of a rotund gentleman with a bushy mustache, who was a frequent guest in my father's house. He was an executive of a railroad car manufacturing company in the east, and he came "out to Kansas City" to visit the Fillmores and discuss metaphysics. He called grandfather "Cholly" and me "Little Cholly." My cousin and I loved to play in the vicinity of his lively discussions with my grandfather, uncle, and father because the atmosphere was always charged with electric good humor and, sooner or later, treats were served to everyone. His hearty laugh and generous spirit were always welcome.

50th anniversary picnic, July 4, 1939

Dedication of the "new" Administration building, New Year's Eve 1915

Lowell (left), Royal (center), Rickert (right)

A most inspiring demonstration of faith in the Jesus Christ principles as presented by Unity was made by a delicately beautiful lady who lived what she believed. She first came to the Fillmores' Sunday classes as a child, found her rightful place, and spent the rest of her life practicing and sharing her extraordinary spiritual discernment. While quite young, she worked in the Unity offices, showing special editorial talent from the start. She married, bore two lovely daughters, and reluctantly left Unity service when her husband's job took the family east. Despite fragile health, she cared for her family and continued to write articles for the publications as well as a number of excellent books on Truth. During her middle years, she faced a serious physical challenge, with doctors offering little hope for her recovery. Her tremendous faith and will to overcome brought her back to health, and when her husband was reassigned to the Midwest, she resumed her editorial work at the School and guided a major Unity publication to its largest circulation ever. It is truly said that to know her was to admire, respect, and love her.

These are but a few of many, many men and women who have helped guide Unity's course during the past century. The movement has never been overly concerned about gaining large numbers through hard-sell proselyting, being content to reach new students through publication, word of mouth, and real-life demonstration. Thus, our first 100 years have been years of slow but steady growth.

When asked what the next century holds for Unity, my answer is that I believe the message will continue to attract intelligent, progressive, positive-minded people. Thus, the future holds unlimited promise for continuity and expansion. Our spiritual movement will not be confined by the limits of a dogma etched in stone, because freedom of spiritual thought breaks all barriers of negation. You who read this are invited to join us as we celebrate our first 100 years of faith in a God of love, whose will is ever-increasing good for all His creation.

Charles R. Fillmore

Myrtle Fillmore (circa 1920)

Our Resolutions

Charles Fillmore

Out of the sordid, the base, the untrue,
Into the noble, the pure, and the new;
Out of all darkness and sadness and sin,
Spiritual harmonies to win.
This is our resolution.

Out of all discord, toil, and strife,
Into a calm and perfect life;
Out of all hatred and jealous fear,
Into love's cloudless atmosphere.
This is our resolution.

Out of the narrow and cramping creeds,
Into a service of loving deeds;
Out of a separate, limited plan,
Into the brotherhood of man.
This is our resolution.

Out of our weakness to conscious
power,
Wisdom and strength for every hour;
Out of our doubt and sore dismay,
Into the faith for which we pray.
This is our resolution.

Out of the bondage of sickness and pain,
Out of poverty's galling chain;
Into the freedom of perfect health,
Into the blessings of endless wealth.
This is our resolution.

Out of this fleeting mortal breath,
Out of the valley and shadow of death;
Into the light of the perfect way,
Into the freedom of endless day.
This is our resolution.

Out of the finite sense of things,
Into the joy the infinite brings;
Out of the limits of time and space,
Into the boundless life of the race.
This is our resolution.

Charles Fillmore (circa 1930)

The Beginning

428 Elmwood, Kansas City, Missouri; Royal (left), Lowell (center), and Myrtle (circa 1920)

James Dillet Freeman
Unity's "Poet Laureate"

Charles Fillmore began his magazine, *Modern Thought*, which became *Unity*, in 1889. This is considered Unity's official birthdate. Myrtle Fillmore began the Society of Silent Help, which became Silent Unity, in 1890.

No one knows the exact date, but it probably was in 1885 or 1886 that the Fillmores went to a lecture by a Dr. E. B. Weeks, who had been sent to Kansas City by a metaphysical teacher, Emma Curtis Hopkins, who had a school of metaphysics in Chicago. Charles later told friends that the lecture had no effect on him, but when Myrtle came out of the hall, she was repeating to herself the words: *I am a child of God and therefore I do not inherit sickness.*

Myrtle Fillmore went home, threw away her medicines, and began to realize that truly she was a child of God; she was made in His image and likeness, and therefore, she too, must be perfect. She began to affirm this truth for herself, to speak words of healing to her mind and body, and in a short time she was healed.

When friends and neighbors saw her gain healing for herself, they asked her to pray with them. This she was glad to do. She was overflowing with the jubilant realization that she was a child of God and therefore perfect in every way, and she was confident that what was true for her was true for all. She would meet with those who asked her to pray with them, speak words of faith and strength to them, and lead them in declaring affirmations of Truth for themselves. In a short time, people were finding healing by joining in prayer with Myrtle Fillmore.

So we might very truly say that it was in the prayers of Myrtle Fillmore for her own healing and for the healing of those who came to her and asked for help that Unity and Silent Unity really began. We chose the date of the publication of the magazine, *Modern Thought*, April 1889, to mark the official beginning of the Unity movement because it provides us with a definite and fixed date. But we know that several years of spiritual ministry preceded this.

Early Unity workers (circa 1912)

The Tracy Avenue complex, Kansas City, Missouri, Publishing entrance (circa 1923)

Unity mail truck (circa 1930)

Summer school leaders and teachers (circa 1920)

It was in 1891 that the Fillmores gave the name of *Silent Unity* to the prayer ministry they had been calling the Society of Silent Help, and the name *Unity* to their entire movement, for which until then, they had no name. Before this, they had simply said that they were teaching practical Christianity.

Charles Fillmore was not one to take things on blind faith. He had an inquiring, scientific turn of mind. When he saw the healings that were coming as a result of his wife's prayers, he began to question why they should come to pass. If people were being healed, there was a reason for the healings. He commenced to inquire into this reason. He read all the books that he could find on the subject, and where courses were available, he took them.

At first Mr. Fillmore was disturbed by the many conflicting statements about Truth made by various teachers. He could not understand why there should be so many divisions and schools and such an assortment of opinions about an exact science. "The muddle was so deep," he wrote, "that for a time I was inclined to ridicule, yet I couldn't get away from the evidence of a great power back of the flood of contradictory statements."

A window at 917 Tracy, Kansas City, Missouri (present day)

There might be doubt as to which of the teachers was right, but as to the results there could be no doubt whatever. His eyes could see the results. About his doubt he wrote:

"I noticed, however, that all the teachers and writers talked a great deal about the omnipresent, omniscient God, who is Spirit and accessible to everyone. I said to myself, 'In this babel I will go to headquarters. If I am Spirit and this God they talk so much about is Spirit, we can somehow communicate, or the whole thing is a fraud.'

"I then commenced sitting in the silence every night at a certain hour and tried to get in touch with God. There was no enthusiasm about it; no soul desire, but a cold, calculating business method. I was there on time every night and tried in all conceivable ways to realize that my mind was in touch with the Supreme Mind.

"In this cold, intellectual attitude one can easily understand why I did not seem to get any conscious result, but I kept at it month after month, mentally affirming words that others told me would open the way, until it got to be a habit and I rather enjoyed it.

"However, a time came when I began to observe that I was having exceedingly realistic dreams. For months I paid no attention to them, my business at that time being of the earth earthy—buying and selling real estate. The first connection that I observed between the dreams and my affairs was after closing the purchase of a piece of property I remembered that I had dreamed about the whole transaction some months before.

"After that I watched my dreams closely and found that there was a wider intelligence manifesting in my sleep than I seemed to possess in the waking state, and it flashed over me one day that this was the mode of communication that had been established in response to my desire for information from headquarters. This has been kept up ever since with growing

Foggy morning on Unity lakeshore

interest on my part, and I could fill a large book with my experiences.

"Everything which it is necessary for me to know is shown to me, and I have times without number been saved from false steps by this monitor. Again and again, I have had mapped out the future along certain lines for months and years ahead, and the prophecies have so far never failed, although I have sometimes misinterpreted the symbols which are used."

This was the way in which Charles Fillmore came into Truth. Being practical, he sought something that was an exact science. Being a student, he studied under many teachers. In the end he turned, as must all who seek Truth, to the one true Source.

Who had the original idea that resulted in Silent Unity—whether it was Charles or Myrtle or some member of the group who was working with them in preparing their magazine and teaching their classes—we do not know. Most of us who have been part of Unity for a long while have always felt that the idea was probably Myrtle's. She was the one who first announced that spiritual communion is not limited by the limitations of space.

The moment that the announcement of the Society of Silent Help was made in 1890, people began to write in, asking the little group in Kansas City to pray with them.

The requirements for joining Silent Unity were

Silent Unity healing meeting (circa 1960)

Peace Chapel entrance, Unity Village

Unity Village retreatants "greet the sun."

and still are simple. You wrote or called Silent Unity, then you spent time each day praying with them, meditating on the same thought that "the little band" in Kansas City was holding in mind.

Here are the two ideas that made Silent Unity the worldwide spiritual ministry it is:

One, *prayer*.

Two, *united prayer*.

If there is one word that has always signified Silent Unity, the word is *prayer*. The Fillmores and their fellow workers prayed. They studied prayer; they practiced prayer; they prayed for themselves; they prayed for others; they prayed.

Charles Fillmore wrote in one of the first issues of *Modern Thought* that he had found God by going to "headquarters," that is, by praying. He told friends that he spent from four to six hours every day in prayer and meditation. He followed this practice all his life.

But just as clearly as the Fillmores saw the power in prayer, they saw the unbelievable, miraculous power in united prayer. They accepted literally the statement of Jesus, "Where two or three are gathered in my name, there am I in the midst of them."

Charles Fillmore's decision to call his movement Unity was an inspired one, for he and Myrtle had an extraordinary sense of the unity of all human beings. They sensed that no one can pray for himself alone. The closer we draw to the center of our own being, the closer we draw to God, for God is the center of our being. And the closer we draw to God, the closer we draw to one another. When anyone is lifted up in prayer, everyone who is linked in thought with him is lifted up, too.

James D. Wit Freeman

The Essence of Unity

The Fillmores' experiences with prayer have, over the past century, evolved into a core of ideas that are the essence of Unity teachings on prayer.

Principles of Affirmative Prayer

It is important to understand that God is Spirit rather than person, place, or thing. When we think of God as a person-like being, we limit the power of God to work in our lives because God as Spirit acts *through* us rather than *upon* us. If we see God in terms of human characteristics, God becomes (to us) a limited and arbitrary being who sometimes answers prayer and sometimes does not. God is not subject to conflicting thoughts and emotions as we are. God is an unchanging and ever-present principle of absolute good.

God is the creative source of all life. God's true nature is Spirit; therefore, humankind's true nature, as God's offspring, is spiritual. As creative beings, our minds are the creators of our world, the realm of earthly manifestation. God creates in the realm of ideas, and humankind forms these ideas into manifestation through thoughts and words. As expressions of God, we are given dominion over earthly manifestation; we are the instruments through which God's greater good comes forth and expresses in the visible world. With this understanding, our highest prayer becomes the desire to be a channel for more of God's good to flow into the world.

"We can best understand our true relationship with God by becoming aware of the Christ idea within ourselves."

Our Relationship With God

We can best understand our true relationship with God by becoming aware of the Christ idea within ourselves. The Christ idea is the seed within us that contains the perfect pattern of wholeness that Jesus Christ exemplified. The man, Jesus of Nazareth, became a fully evolved expression of this divine idea called *the Christ*, and through His life and teachings, He shows us the way to the realization of the Christ potential within us. Prayer links us in a very personal way with God and awakens in us the realization of our true relationship.

Our Inheritance: Divine Ideas

Our inheritance is available to us at all times in the form of divine ideas. Divine ideas are created within God-Mind. These living, eternal ideas of perfect good work through our minds to become manifest good in the world. Charles Fillmore taught that there are twelve main divine ideas (symbolized by the twelve disciples of Jesus) from which all others spring. They are: *faith*, *strength*, *wisdom*, *love*, *imagination*, *power*, *understanding*, *will*, *order*, *zeal*, *renunciation*, and *life*. The Christ idea is the composite divine idea containing all possible ideas of perfect good for humankind. In prayer, we claim our inheritance of divine ideas and set in motion the creative process that clothes them with substance and draws them into the realm of visibility. Our goal in prayer is to realize our sonship, to claim our gifts of divine ideas, and to allow them to come forth as manifest good through our unwavering faith in the creative power of God.

One Mind

We connect with God through our minds. Our minds may appear to be separate from God, yet, in reality, this is not so. There is only one mind, one intelligence, operating in the universe, and that mind is God. Each person, as an offspring of God, is an individualized expression of universal Mind. The awareness that we are never separate from God in mind allows us to consciously link with the one Mind by turning our attention Godward in prayer. This common bond makes it possible for us to effectively pray for others as well as for ourselves.

The Law of Mind Action

The law of mind action is the process through which divine ideas in Mind express through the human mind and out into the manifest realm. Through the action of this law, the attitudes and beliefs we hold in our minds will eventually come forth in our earthly experience. It is important to continually experience positive prayer and to dwell on God's ideas of perfect good, for this law will express any thoughts we hold in mind whether they are negative or positive.

"There is only one mind, one intelligence, operating in the universe, and that mind is God."

15

The more we realize our sonship and claim God's gifts of divine ideas, the more God's good will automatically be expressed in the world. This is why Jesus advised to "seek first his kingdom . . . ." As we seek to realize our oneness with God and desire only God's good gifts, such as life, love, and abundance, the law of mind action will work to create greater health, greater peace, and greater prosperity in our lives.

Because the creative activity of God, through the law of mind action, is always at work bringing into expression our innermost thoughts and feelings, our words become powerful tools for drawing forth good or ill in our lives. Our words are so powerful because they express in a concrete way our thoughts and beliefs about ourselves and our world. In prayer, we use the power of our words to both cleanse and uplift our consciousness of Truth. We use denials to say "no" to limited beliefs we may hold that are based on a false concept of separation from God and God's good. We use affirmations to say "yes" to the Truth that we are spiritual beings, beloved sons and daughters of a loving and giving Father-Mother God. Prayer that recognizes and declares this Truth is called *affirmative prayer*. Affirmative prayer is based on the realization of Sonship, the acceptance of divine ideas as our inheritance, and steadfast faith in the unfailing operation of divine law.

The Purpose of Prayer

Prayer is the process of turning our full attention to the Christ potential within us in an attempt to experience God's presence and power. Communing with God is our first purpose in prayer. Our second purpose in prayer is to recognize that as children of God we are heirs to God's freely given gifts of divine ideas and their resulting manifestations of good. In prayer we begin to understand that these gifts are always available to us

"We are not so much seeking to reach God as to express God."

and that we are the channels through which these ideas express in the world. Therefore, it is our responsibility to claim the gifts of the kingdom and to draw them into manifestation.

In prayer, we seek God until we are lifted up by the very presence and power we are seeking. This is why Jesus said that all those who seek will find. We can be assured of finding God through prayer because that which we seek is already available to us. We are not so much seeking to *reach* God as to *express* God as life, love, intelligence, power, and substance. Our prayers do not change God, they change our *awareness* of God. Prayer increases our understanding of God's true nature as Spirit, the unchanging presence of all good. Prayer uplifts our conscious awareness of the truth of our being and, therefore, opens us to all the good in God-Mind for our use.

Types of Prayer

The process of turning our attention to God in prayer can be approached in many different ways. In Unity, we combine prayers of invocation with prayers of affirmation, acknowledging both the transcendent and immanent aspects of God. When we use both asking and affirmative prayer forms, we establish a balanced understanding of God's true nature as loving presence in life and as unfailing principle of creative law. These two forms of prayer involve both our feeling and thinking natures in the prayer process. Meditation and concentration are *techniques* we use in prayer to help us attain the realization of God we seek. There are many types of meditation and concentration methods used in the various spiritual disciplines of the world. In Unity, the purpose of these techniques is primarily to focus the attention on God. Denials and affirmations are *tools* that we use within our minds to help bring about a realization of God as all-providing Source. Through the use of denials we remove error thoughts from our consciousness and cleanse our belief system of any belief that limits God's power to act in our lives. We use affirmations to claim the Truth and to draw it forth into visibility.

The Silence

Unity's prayer method is called "the silence." We enter the silence to consciously experience our oneness within the one Mind, God. To do so we must change the focus of our minds; we must withdraw our attention from the manifest realm of effects and turn inward where we seek and find the cause of all things, God as Spirit. God's presence in all its fullness is always available to us, for it is in, around, and through us.

We must, however, turn to God in the silence in order for this Truth to be revealed to us. For this revelation to come about, we need to learn to disengage from our everyday consciousness, which is focused primarily in the realms of sensation, thought, and feeling. By detaching ourselves from these areas of consciousness, we enter the intuitive faculty of our minds and discover there our link with God: "the secret place of the most high." The secret place of the most high is the place in consciousness where God is directly experienced, where *believing* becomes *knowing*, where the concept of the Christ within becomes a personal reality. In the secret place we accomplish our goal in prayer by realizing God as the all-providing Father-Mother presence, All Good.

Within the secret place of the most high we listen for the "still small voice" of God. This voice is not a sound but rather a feeling of inner knowing and peace. All of us must learn to contact the voice of God within ourselves and become accustomed to it. This inner voice comes from the silence within us, and it will

"God's presence in all its fullness is always available to us."

teach us exactly what we need to know and do to unfold spiritually. The still small voice will direct and guide us in definite ways once we learn to hear and trust it. To contact the voice of God, we must wait upon the Lord in the silence.

When we are comfortable and relaxed, the process of detaching from a normal state of consciousness can begin. It is therefore important to take the time needed to prepare the environment, body, and consciousness for entering the silence. Once we have disengaged from our everyday consciousness, we turn our full attention to God by meditating and concentrating on words or ideas of Truth. We may dwell upon divine ideas or aspects of God such as love, life, peace, health, or substance. Or, we may simply focus on words of Truth that invoke a realization of God's love such as "God Is, I Am" or "Peace, be still." Whatever technique we use, the purpose is the same—to lead us into the secret place, a state of consciousness where we commune with God, to realize our sonship, and to claim the gifts of the kingdom.

Affirmative Prayer

Affirmative prayer is prayer that recognizes the eternal reality of divine ideas and humankind as the vehicle through which these ideas become manifest. Divine ideas in God-Mind are brought forth through human minds and are expressed in the world by the unalterable law of mind action. Access to divine ideas and the creative process as law are God's gifts to humankind. We then pray affirmatively to become channels for the expression of God in the manifest realm in which we live. Whatever we are praying for, whether it is healing, guidance, love, or prosperity, it is always available to us, not as *things* but as *ideas* with the potential to become manifest in our lives.

It is our responsibility to recognize and affirm this Truth in thought, word, and deed. As we do so, we claim our divine inheritance.

Denials and Affirmations

Denials and affirmations are tools we use to bring about a realization of Truth. When we use denials we remove negative and limiting thoughts from our consciousness; we say "no" to the power of false beliefs or negative conditions to block our good from coming forth. When we use affirmations, we claim our gifts from God; we say "yes" to the activity of divine ideas in our life. Denials and affirmations are not magic words. The words themselves have no power to change outer circumstances. Their power lies in their ability to transform our consciousness of God.

Negative conditions lose their power in our lives because we are no longer holding them in place with our mental energy. Instead, we are focusing on the good. Therefore, the good must come forth according to law. The process of using cleansing denials and claiming affirmations is ongoing. We must continue to speak these words of Truth silently and audibly until a realization of the Truth is experienced. When the necessary shift from error belief to Truth belief takes place in consciousness—then, and only then—outer circumstances begin to change for the better.

Our minds are never separate from God, yet, ignorance of this Truth can make us believe falsely that we are separated from our source of good. Negative conditions are not permanent, nor do they have power equal to, or stronger than, God's power of good. They are simply errors, false beliefs and illusions that have come into manifestation. They are created through the same law—the law of mind action—that also brings forth good. The law is a servant to the mind; it will eventually manifest

Administration building, Unity Village

whatever type of thoughts are held there. Because they have no life, substance, or intelligence of their own to sustain them, negative conditions dissolve when we change the focus of our thought from the illusion of separation from God to the Truth of oneness with God. Denials uproot error beliefs and eliminate the source of negativity in mind.

It is important to remember that the work must be done in consciousness before a demonstration of truth can become visible. Jesus said, "You will know them by their fruits" (Mt. 7:16).

We know our prayers are effective when we see a change for the better in the manifest realm. Thus, we must persist in affirmative prayer for health until health is demonstrated, for illumination until guidance is clear, for supply until greater supply comes forth, for love until love is experienced. As our realization of truth comes forth within our minds, we will be guided to whatever action we need to take for the perfect unfoldment of our answered prayer. Our part is to pray affirmatively, to know the Truth about the situation, and to allow the Spirit of Truth to lead us to the perfect fulfillment of our desire.

Balance

In prayer, we understand God as principle so that we may pray affirmatively and be assured of answered prayer. However, we also need to cultivate a personal relationship with the Lord of our being. When we realize that God is both principle and personal, both law and love, we bring to our times of prayer a balance of thought and feeling. This balance will help to lead us more easily into the secret place of the most high where we can experience our oneness with God.

A personal realization of oneness with God is built around the composite divine idea of the Christ within. In order to achieve this, it is necessary first to understand and then experience that seed of perfection, the Christ pattern of wholeness that exists within our own being. By seeking an intimate, intuitive realization of the Christ consciousness in prayer, we become united with God in a deeply personal way. Through the realization that we, too, are literally children of God, we claim our status as joint heirs with our brother and Way-Shower, Jesus Christ.

The Goal

Ella Wheeler Wilcox

All roads that lead to God are good;
What matters it, your faith or mine;
Both center at the goal divine
Of love's eternal brotherhood.

A thousand creeds have come and gone;
But what is that to you or me?
Creeds are but branches of a tree,
The root of love lives on and on.

Though branch by branch proves withered
     wood,
The root is warm with precious wine;
Then keep your faith, and leave me mine;
All roads that lead to God are good.

Silent Unity Today

John A. V. Strickland
Director of Silent Unity

Silent Unity's main purpose remains as it has throughout the history of Unity—prayer. Much more takes place in Silent Unity than "formal" prayer, but our mission is prayer. We believe that any steps we must take in the outer are actually prayer in action.

We begin our work each day with prayer as we share the *Daily Word* lesson. Afterward, the Mail Opening Department has a time of prayer over the mail that came in that morning. We have a prayer time we call the Healing Meeting at 11 a.m. Then, after lunch, we have a time of prayer before beginning the afternoon work. On most Thursday afternoons, we have a prosperity meeting with a ministerial student.

Each of the eight-hour shifts in the Telephone Prayer Room has a time of prayer before taking over the telephone duty. This is in addition to a constant vigil of prayer 24 hours a day in a special room. Here, a Silent Unity employee sits in prayer for a half-hour period, and then is replaced by another worker. We involve ourselves also in special prayer projects, study projects, and other consciousness-raising activities throughout the year. While we maintain our mission of devoted, loving prayer, we also study, learn, grow, and pray for each other.

Silent Unity Today

"Hello, this is Silent Unity. How may we help you?" If you have ever called Silent Unity, you have probably heard these or similar words. More than 650,000 times this year, our telephones will ring and we will be here for you. The workers in Silent Unity stand ready, willing, and able to pray with callers 24 hours a day, 7 days a week, 365 days a year. We do not judge callers; we do not try to convert callers; we do not solicit donations over the telephone. We simply listen, behold the Christ in the caller and all that concerns him or her, and speak the affirmative word of Truth. We are not a counseling service. We are simply a power-filled, Spirit-filled, dedicated band of employees, who will pray with anyone, anytime, for God's blessings to be made manifest in any situation.

Phone Room (circa 1940)

"Every letter receives a prayer blessing." (circa 1930)

"We have received an astounding 52,000 letters in a single day!"

Silent Unity handles every piece of correspondence that comes to Unity Village.

Every letter receives a prayer blessing whether or not the correspondent is specifically writing to Silent Unity for prayer help. As incredible as it may seem, Silent Unity receives more than 2.7 million letters each year. We have received an astounding 52,000 letters in a single day! Each letter is read individually and responded to with love and efficiency.

We consider it a sacred responsibility and a great privilege to be called to serve in this capacity. We are ordinary people who believe in God and in the power of prayer, and we are privileged to behold extraordinarily good results in the lives of great numbers of people as a result.

We have a fine publishing ministry here at Unity School, and we give thanks for it. One Unity publication we in Silent Unity claim as our own—*Daily Word* magazine. Each month Unity mails *Daily Word* (in English) to nearly three million homes around the world. *Daily Word* is translated into nine other languages. *La Palabra Diaria*, the Spanish edition of *Daily Word*, and *Daily Word in Large Type* are published and distributed by Unity School.

Daily Word is Silent Unity's way of keeping in contact with our friends in almost 160 countries. It reminds us of our worldwide mission of prayer, and it reminds our friends to pray with us while we are praying with them. We believe that this pocket-sized publication is a vehicle of Truth—ordained by God, we might say. From Christians, Jews, Hindus, Buddhists, Moslems, and those who claim other religions or no religion as their own, we receive reports of improved lives. Some tell us that they could not begin their day without first reading *Daily Word*. Therefore, we make every effort to give the best service possible.

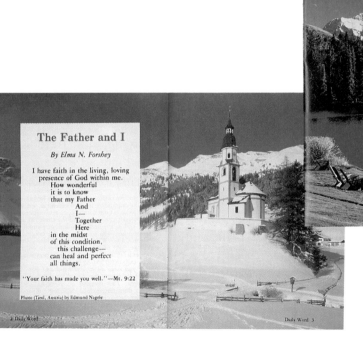

"With the advent of computers, we can give more personal attention to greater numbers of people."

"Does Silent Unity use computers?" some may ask. Yes, indeed. We do not use computers to read the mail or to pray with our friends. However, we make use of the latest technology available to ensure that our magazines are sent to the correct addresses in a timely manner, that our letters are typed perfectly, and that address changes are handled correctly. Computers also help us prepare our pamphlets and prayer cards.

We live in the twentieth century, we use the finest equipment that we can acquire, and we hire the most dedicated workers we can find. Four million people are actively involved with Unity. We could not keep up with all the prayer requests, address changes, or magazine and book orders without the assistance of modern data-processing equipment. With the advent of computers, we have found that we can give more personal attention to greater numbers of people. It is true that we have been able to devote more attention to each prayer request since we entered the computer age nearly 20 years ago. Machines do the mundane tasks so that more people may pray.

Spirit has guided us in our work since it began, and we are fortunate that, as the requests for prayer have increased, so has our ability to respond with the personal, loving touch, using the best technology available.

Silent Unity answers millions of letters and telephone calls each year. We work with the latest technology to give the best possible service, but we emphasize that first, last, and always our work is prayer.

Truly, Silent Unity is a dedicated ministry of prayer. It is more than 250 people who work in the Silent Unity building at Unity Village. Silent Unity is a worldwide prayer consciousness. We gladly welcome all people who believe in God and the power of prayer into our household of faith. We are Silent Unity, and you are part of us. We are grateful for the wonder-working power of prayer!

John A. V. Strickland

A glimpse of the new Silent Unity building

Construction of the new Silent Unity building proceeds
quickly. (1988)

Unity Visits With Friends

During most of its 100 years, Unity's greatest outreach to people around the world has been through mail and the telephone. Millions of letters and phone calls flow in and out of the School each year to assist Truth students with prayer requests. As one of the Midwest's largest publishers, Unity provides its readers with a variety of magazines, books, and study guides, designed to offer spiritual and inspirational encouragement to those who write to Unity for help.

From the earliest days of Unity, the prayer ministry, Silent Unity, has maintained what appears to be an impersonal, anonymous approach to prayer. Letters and phone calls are received and prayed over with sensitivity and dedication by the workers in Silent Unity. Often, a Unity friend or correspondent will want to know the name of the worker in Silent Unity who has so lovingly responded to a prayer request or other need. This is not Silent Unity's way. All requests for help receive the same attention from the Silent Unity worker who might be praying with and for you.

In the summer of 1984 Unity School embarked on one of its most ambitious projects. To better meet the growing needs of those across the country and around the world who look to Silent Unity for prayer help, it became necessary to expand the facilities and outreach possibilities of Silent Unity. To do so, Unity's Board of Trustees announced a $14,000,000 Revenue Generation program to construct a new building and home for Silent Unity.

In only two years, the necessary funds from more than 300,000 generous donors were received. Throughout that time, some Unity employees, while traveling on School business around the country, were encouraged to personally visit and express appreciation to people who have made Unity a part of their lives for many years.

These personal calls were well received and appreciated. The visits also gave Unity a better understanding of the people it serves.

These visits revealed many beautifully inspiring stories of how Unity has helped individuals in their daily lives. One of the most extraordinary discoveries was the opportunity to see how diverse the Unity family is. For instance, Unity friends are found among nearly every religious denomination in the country. A significant percentage have read and studied Unity publications for 50 years or more.

"New" friends visit in the Fellowship lounge.

We are happy to share here some of their stories.

A retired chief executive officer of one of America's largest energy companies told of his initial contact with Unity through reading *Daily Word* as a youngster. While still a student, he discovered that all things were possible for a person who followed the basic, practical teachings of Jesus Christ. He started with his company as a stock boy and rose through the ranks to become chairman of the board. "Not only did Unity's teachings help me in my daily, personal life, but I found that I was using Unity's philosophy in every decision I was expected to make in behalf of my company's employees, management, and shareholders alike. I attribute so much of my success to Unity, and I am grateful."

One of America's outstanding philanthropists and patrons of the arts recalled that she has not missed one morning of

The new Silent Unity building—view from the Education building

Unity If

Nita Buckley

If I can know that God is omnipotent
  When others doubt that He is true,
If I can touch that part of God within me
  And see the Christ abide in others too,
If I can pray and not be tired by prayer
  Or, being weary, not begin to doubt,
If the candle of my faith begins to flicker
  And I can keep the flame from going out,
If I can draw upon sustaining power
  To help me cope and meet my needs each
    day
If I can be a comfort and give guidance
  And help another person find his way,

If I can tap the knowledge of omniscience
  And reach into the heart of Divine Mind,
If I can ease the grief of someone hurting
  And offer words of hope for all mankind,
If I can walk with the corrupt without
    corruption
  And see God where it seems that evil lies,
If I can stand with courage and decision
  And keep the goal steadfast before my
    eyes,
If I can fill a heavy heart with laughter
  And recognize that joy is mine to share
And see the pattern of my highest good
    unfolding,
  I'm living in my Father's loving care.

The Peace Chapel

The Publishing Ministry

William B. Dale
Vice President/Publishing
Unity School of Christianity

The celebration of a century of service is an important and exciting event in the life of an organization. It is especially meaningful for those of us serving in the publishing ministry, since the official birth date of the Unity movement is the date Unity School of Christianity published the first issue of a magazine titled *Modern Thought*. Those first sixteen pages of print in April 1889, have evolved into a multitude of magazines, books, pamphlets, brochures, and other printed material. Each is designed and written to meet the spiritual needs of those who turn to Unity for help.

In the early years, all the publishing work, except the actual printing, was done in the home of Charles and Myrtle Fillmore. As the work grew, space was rented in various buildings in Kansas City and the operational responsibility for publishing was entrusted to other dedicated workers. Also, Unity purchased its own sheetfed printing presses. By the close of the first decade of the twentieth century, Unity School was constructing its own building at 917 Tracy in Kansas City to house, among other departments, the publishing activities.

43

Tracy Avenue Printing Plant, Kansas City, Missouri (circa 1923)

Tracy Avenue Publishing Plant exterior, Kansas City, Missouri (circa 1928)

In 1948, the publishing work was relocated to its present site in Unity Village. By the mid-1970's the printing volume had outgrown the capacity of the sheetfed presses. The decision was made to move all the press work to outside firms, firms that could provide a wider choice of equipment, including high-speed web presses, to more economically produce monthly the millions of pieces of literature. The editorial, art, photography, and typesetting functions as well as the binding and mailing, continued to be performed at Unity Village.

Over the years every effort has been made to provide an optimum of balance relating to the quality and economy of printing. Special care has always been taken in the selection of manuscripts, art, photographs, paper, and equipment to provide the most appropriate printed communications for the Unity teachings. In its 100-year history, seven leaders of the publishing ministry have followed the Fillmores. Each of my predecessors, W. T. Smith, William Whitworth, John Chesnutt, John Garrison, Alex Alberg, and Claborn Brants, endeavored to faithfully adhere to the standards of quality in publishing established by the Fillmores. I am honored to continue that legacy of commitment to excellence.

Setting type the hard way

"Charles and Myrtle Fillmore envisioned the publishing activities of Unity School as a ministry from inception."

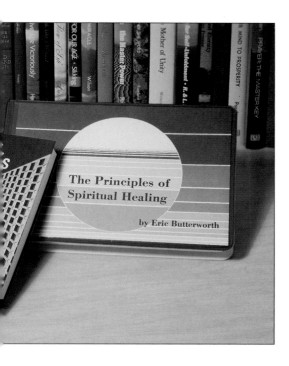

I still recall the fascination of first seeing the literature being printed, bound, and mailed in the Publishing Plant. It was in 1971 when I arrived in Unity Village to enter the ministerial training program. The aroma of the ink and the rhythmic sounds of the presses combined with the motion of all the cutting, folding, stitching, and inserting equipment to create an awesome atmosphere. My feelings of appreciation for the wonderful work being done there were strengthened. Little did I realize that my personal ministry was later to be so satisfyingly expressed through publishing.

Lowell Fillmore was president emeritus of Unity School when I came to the Village. During the next several years prior to his passing, Lowell frequently visited the area where I worked and joined in our morning prayer and meditation time using the *Daily Word*. He often shared stories of his early years at Unity School helping his mother and father. Many of Lowell's recollections have been recorded in print. One story recalled his part in publishing when the Unity work was in its infancy. "When the work was in the house on McGee Street many things that I did as part of the daily routine and that took me just a few minutes to do alone constitute whole departments now. I ran the small job press, printed the envelopes and stationery and helped write the letters.

Current shipping facilities at Unity Village

Tracy Avenue Shipping Department, Kansas City, Missouri (circa 1928)

"I was also the order-filling department. I often found that we were out of some of our books, which had been printed but not yet folded or bound. So I would go and get the printed sheets of paper, fold them by hand, get them ready, and stitch them and trim them. We kept our finished stock in the office in the front room; the printed pages, covers, binding materials, and other things in the pantry of the old house. I would wrap and stamp the books and take them to the post office.

"I don't believe that Father or Mother realized in those days how the work was going to grow. That is, they felt that they had been told by Spirit to do this work, and that it was a great work, but they never planned or thought how big it might become."

Today more than 100 people serve in the various departments of the publishing ministry, preparing and mailing Unity literature and materials. The departments of Purchasing, Editorial, Graphic Arts, and Publishing Plant work as a team to produce millions of printed pieces and

"Unity mailings are received by people in 160 countries."

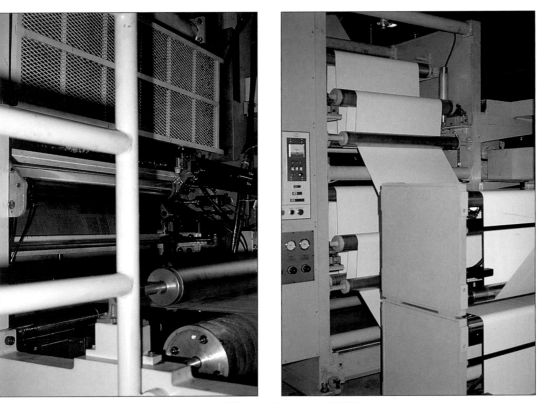

Modern high tech presses now print much of Unity's literature. (1988)

Vile-Goller Fine Arts Printing and Litho-Graphing (1988)

Publishing Plant at Unity Village (1988)

hundreds of thousands of books and audiovisual materials annually. Scores of paper mills throughout the United States produce the tons of fine quality printing paper purchased to supply Unity's needs. Five local printing firms utilizing dozens of high technology machines print Unity School's material. Here in Unity Village, high-speed equipment designed especially for Unity School is used in the binding and mailing operations. The output of the plant averages more than 300,000 pieces of mail each working day. Unity mailings now are received by people in 160 countries.

Charles and Myrtle Fillmore envisioned the publishing activities of Unity School as a ministry from inception. That concept is being continued today. The providing of inspirational literature, audiocassettes, and videocassettes to millions throughout the world is indeed an active and effective ministry.

49

Unity Lake

Charles and Myrtle Fillmore were avid readers. In fact, they met at a literary club meeting, where they discovered one another's interest in classic literature and in the power of the printed word. So it is not surprising that a large part of the work they would establish together would involve publishing.

Early in his efforts to understand the apparently miraculous changes taking place in his wife and in others with whom she prayed, Charles spent a great deal of time reading and studying anything he could find relating to healing, prayer, spirituality, and the power of the mind. It occurred to him that there was an awfully lot of disconnected and discordant information. He felt that all these people should know about one another and share their insights, experiences, and revelations. His practical sense knew that in all the confusion there must be some common ground, and he intended to find and share it. So in 1889 he began to publish *Modern Thought*.

In its infancy, *Modern Thought* was devoted mostly to discussions of physical healing. Likely, this was because the Fillmores' entry into the study of Truth was precipitated by Myrtle's healing. They became expressly interested in a popular philosophy of the time espoused by Mary Baker Eddy. They were instrumental in spreading the Christian Science teachings through *Modern Thought*. Later they were ordained in Christian Science. But changes were in the offing.

The Fillmores were adamant about the importance of individuals finding Truth for themselves. One must, through personal effort in dedication and prayer, seek to develop one's own relationship with God. It seemed to them that Mrs. Eddy and some of her followers were exhibiting feelings of exclusivity in the revelations of God. They were becoming more dogmatic and possessive of the ideas that the Fillmores believed were free gifts to all who were willing to accept them.

In an unsigned editorial in the July 1889 issue of *Modern Thought*, the writer (probably Charles) expressed consternation at the claims of some Christian Scientists to being "so perfect in soul development as to be always en rapport with the Christ principle, and not subject to any of the influences common to humanity at large . . . . Hence, if we would be wise, we must look for pure men and women, and classify them according to their purity, regardless of the metaphysical or any other line of thought which they represent." Thus, they ceased formal affiliation with Christian Science in order to maintain their integrity of purpose.

In 1891 they began another publication, *Unity* magazine, which was comprised of some of the articles published in *Modern Thought*. But it was much shorter and devoted specifically to those interested in the healing prayer work of the Society of Silent Unity. Then in 1895 *Modern Thought* and *Unity* magazine were merged once again.

Although the Fillmores never wavered from their desire not to create another religion, from the beginning they were certain that the Bible, and particularly the teachings of Jesus Christ, must be the primary source of timeless wisdom and must somehow have practical value in modern society. They saw Jesus not as just a religious figure but as a physical example of spiritual principle. So more and more refinement in their publication took place. Eventually that which was not practical and did not pertain to the Jesus Christ teachings was eliminated.

Ever aware of the public demand for Truth teachings in relation to specific human needs, Unity experimented with various types of publications. There was *The Christian Business Man* (later *Christian Business*, then *Good Business*), which taught the value of applying spiritual principles in business. Charles, having been a businessman before he was caught up in the work of Unity, felt that spiritual principles certainly had a place in the business world.

There was also *Youth* (later *Y.O.U.*, then *Progress*), which approached the spiritual life from the viewpoint of the younger set, those not yet adults but no longer children.

There were others, such as *Weekly Unity* and *New* magazine. All of these were eventually merged into the current *Unity* magazine.

The *Unity* magazine of today is of quite a different character from the early issues. It carries no advertisements except those of Unity products and services. Its purpose is to "help people understand their own spiritual nature and to express spirituality in their lives in practical ways" (from Unity's Statement of Purpose). But the original ideals of individual growth and progress by following the teachings of Jesus Christ have been continued.

In the pages of *Unity* magazine you will find lessons on metaphysical interpretation of the Bible, Bible history and theology by experts in the field, personal accounts of the power of prayer to enhance lives, inspirational articles, poetry, and artwork designed to help busy people become calm and receptive to spiritual ideas. But always, the emphasis is on the practical.

In one recent issue, a woman told how in applying the principle of nonjudgment and forgiveness, her relationship with her daughter was healed of a sad condition the woman had not even known existed until the day when her daughter attempted suicide. This opened the door to

"The Unity *magazine of today is of quite a different character from the early issues . . . but the original ideals have been continued."*

the woman's inner search for Truth as she had never before thought of it.

Another story dealt with a Christian mother's memory of a fear-filled, lonely Christmas Eve. As she sat crying with her critically ill child, life was transformed "miraculously" by the love and compassion of a Jewish rabbi.

Thousands of letters are written to Silent Unity each year, thanking them for praying and telling of the wonders that have occurred in the writers' lives when they have learned to see without fear, to love without judgment, to have faith without evidence, to give without anxiety about return. These are the ideals of Unity and its publications. They are Christ ideals, which we are all capable of attaining. Many of these letters are published in *Unity* magazine so that the "miracles" that occur will continue to inspire and heal as the more than 400,000 subscribers share the writers' joy.

Unity magazine is dedicated to teaching these high values and principles of Truth to individuals throughout the world.

ristmas lights—Administration building, Unity Village
987)

The Presses Keep Rolling

After the Fillmores became acquainted with H. Emilie Cady, whom they considered a superb teacher, they asked her to write some basic lessons for *Unity* magazine. This she did, and the lessons were later compiled into Unity's first and most popular book, *Lessons in Truth*. The Fillmores considered *Lessons in Truth* a "foundation stone" for Unity teachings. This opinion has not changed. More than a million and a half copies have been sold, and it remains on Unity's best-seller list.

Since then, hundreds of titles have been published by Unity. Currently there are more than 100 titles in print, including books on prayer, healing, Unity history, prosperity, theology, Bible stories, uplifting and inspiring fables, and books of inspiration in poetry, song, and essay form.

Great care is taken in the publication of each book. Unity has always maintained a high standard of quality in the content as well as the makeup of a book.

Photography studio sets up an attractive shot for publication.

Actual finished product after all of the elements have been added

Silent Unity Responds

If you have ever called Silent Unity, you have probably received, after a few days, a pamphlet, speaking especially to the need for which you asked Silent Unity to pray with you. This has been a part of the Silent Unity response almost since its inception.

Hundreds of thousands of pamphlets are printed each year. Most of them are written by Silent Unity workers. Some are articles from *Unity* magazine or *Daily Word* because they directly addressed a common need. The dedicated people who answer telephones and letters in Silent Unity listen carefully to your prayer requests. They are ever aware of the changing needs of a changing society. So they watch for common threads, particular needs that seem to grow more common. Then, along with the 24-hour prayer service, they write or compile pamphlets with those needs in mind.

Original Radio Room, Ninth and Tracy, Kansas City, Missouri

Broadcast facilities for WOQ (1924-1934)

64

The pamphlets are usually short articles pointing out practical spiritual ways to cope with and solve personal challenges. They can serve as reminders to those for whom Silent Unity is praying that they are on that special list, that they have a loving, caring friend in Unity. The pamphlet can also be used as a guide to affirmative prayer at times when, in the midst of crisis, it is difficult to take one's attention off the problem, which is a necessity in order to pray affirmatively and to find solutions.

WOQ
UNITY RADIO STATION
OWNED AND OPERATED
BY
UNITY SCHOOL OF CHRISTIANITY
917 TRACY AVENUE
KANSAS CITY, MO.

Hearing the Words of Truth

As early as 1922, Unity expanded its ministry beyond the print media to the airwaves. Radio station WOQ, the oldest licensed broadcast station in the Midwest, carried live talks by Unity speakers. The first, Francis J. Gable, broadcast from the window of a store in downtown Kansas City. In 1924 Unity purchased the station and moved the studio to the 917 Tracy building. In order to air the

The New Kid on the Block

The newest program in the publishing ministry is the video tape. The first Unity videocassette tape, *Words of Jesus*, by Ed Rabel, renowned Unity minister and teacher, is a well structured program interpreting the teachings of Jesus.

In celebration of Unity's Centennial in 1989, Unity produced another videocassette: *On Wings of Truth: The Unity Way to Health, Prosperity, and Love.*

This video features Unity ministers Eric Butterworth, James Dillet Freeman, Dorothy Pierson, Jim Rosemergy, and Sharon Poindexter sharing their enlightened perspectives on a number of key issues related to healing, human relationships, and prosperity.

Also appearing are Charles R. Fillmore, chairman of the board, Connie Fillmore, president of Unity School, and John A. V. Strickland, director of Silent Unity, discussing the spiritual significance and history of the Unity work.

The popular acceptance of videocassettes has opened a new and exciting frontier in Unity's publishing efforts. Once again, Unity is there to answer a need, to fulfill the high calling of carrying forth a tradition of spiritual integrity and high-quality production.

James Dillet Freeman videotaping *On Wings of Truth— The Unity Way to Health, Prosperity, and Love* (1988)

A balloon release added a festive air to a videotaping session.

The Languages of Unity

Through its literature, Unity has reached into the far corners of the world. Not only has it been translated into familiar languages like German, French, Spanish, Japanese, Russian, and Italian, but also into lesser known languages, such as Tamil, Gujarati, Ibo, and Afrikaans. Although most of the translation of the literature takes place within the country where that language is most common, these people write to Unity School to tell of the vast influence its literature has had in their lives.

In *The Story of Unity*, James Dillet Freeman tells the story of a man from Nigeria, who visited the United States many years ago. He discovered Unity literature and took some home with him. His countrymen liked it, and the word spread. Later, a geologist noted that in Nigeria there is even a drumbeat that signifies Unity. Today there are thousands of Unity students throughout Nigeria. The word is spreading over all of Africa.

Unity literature has even been carried behind the Iron Curtain and into China. After all, no matter what language a person speaks, no matter his or her country of origin or what political system within which he or she lives, spiritual matters are spiritually discerned, and Unity's influence is not bound by political systems, geography, or languages.

The Bookstore at Unity Village Visitors Center (1988)

A shipment of books for the Youth of Unity Abiriba Chapter (1973)

In the mid-1800s a young man named Louis was a teacher in an unusual school: he taught blind students. He was blind. His frustrations with the difficulties of learning for these special people, because of the vast amount of literature necessary in the education process, led to his development of a written language especially designed for them. Thus, the braille language came into being.

Unity does not leave these people out of its ministry. All three of the periodicals and many Unity books are now printed in braille and are distributed free to those who need them. Also, Unity produces an audiocassette tape of each *Daily Word* lesson throughout every year. These tapes are also distributed free to the sightless. These people have benefited especially from the audiocassette ministry of Unity. As it grows, so does their world.

Charles Fillmore once wrote: "All . . . who have moved the world to better things have received their inspiration from the Spirit within and have always looked to it for instruction." Unity's publishing ministry never has or will intend to take the place of personal soul-searching and silent communion with God within each individual. What the publishing ministry has and will continue to do is to share the insights into Truth that others have had, to teach the methods and techniques of prayer and meditation that can facilitate the inner search. This is the mission, which will not be accomplished until all people in all lands have revealed to them and through them the living Christ, the hope of glory.

The Teacher

Pamela Yearsley

Those who would be teachers, know this:
If your heart is set upon generously sharing with others
your own knowledge, thereby somehow to enhance their lives,
then know that your gift will not succeed.

For a true teacher does not seek to instill in others
her or his understanding and knowledge;
rather, a true teacher seeks to be an instrument
to stimulate the student's own wisdom.

Do not seek to inspire others; seek to be inspired.
Only by being inspired can you bring inspiration.
For inspiration is not a gift we can give to another.
It is a state of being that magnifies itself in others.

A Ministerial Education Program classroom

Silent Unity employee prayer service, Unity Farm (circa 1929)

72

The Fillmore family (circa 1917)

Therefore, feel not downhearted
because in your own ecstasy of inspiration
others do not seem to share.
Instead, hold steady in your way—
in your own state of being—
and be inspired.

Partake lavishly of your experience and
hold no expectations of others doing so.
In their own time, in their own way
will they feast at the same table.
But let not pride take your hand and lord it over their heads.

Let not your students be to you as the moon
whose light is but a reflection.
But let them be as the stars
whose brilliance shows forth of their own nature.
This is the gift of the teacher.

A refreshing summer rain at the Education building, Unity Village (1988)

The Education Ministry

Students and teachers at an early ordination service

Robert R. Barth
Vice President/Education
Unity School of Christianity

"Unity is a link in the great educational movement inaugurated by Jesus Christ; our objective is to discern the truth in Christianity and prove it. The truth that we teach is not new, neither do we claim special revelations or discovery of new religious principles. Our purpose is to help and teach mankind to use and prove the eternal Truth taught by the Master."

—Charles Fillmore

Spiritual education was important to Charles and Myrtle Fillmore. Myrtle realized its impact when she was healed as a result of her understanding that she did not inherit sickness, that she was a child of God. Throughout his writings, you can find Charles discussing the need to understand and live the Truth in order to have a full, happy, prosperous, and healthy life.

Charles and Myrtle began their education ministry around the turn of the century when they taught classes in spiritual matters. In 1909 they established the Correspondence School, and by 1911 over 2,000 people were enrolled. They eventually established the "Intensive Training School," which lasted

Many classes are held in the Activities Center at Unity Village.

for two weeks each summer. This grew into the Unity Training School, predecessor of the current education program.

Today, the education ministry is known as Unity School for Religious Studies (USRS). USRS was established on December 15, 1980. USRS continues the devotion to the Unity traditions of metaphysical Christianity founded by Charles and Myrtle.

Several departments have been developed in USRS to meet the diverse needs of the Unity movement. These include Unity Village Chapel, the Continuing Education Program (CEP), the Ministerial Education Program (MEP), the Retreat Department, Unity Library, Unity Bookstore, and the Counseling and Resource Center.

The Education Department staf

Activities Center

Unity Village Chapel is the church for Unity Village. It offers Sunday worship services, weekly classes, seminars, workshops, counseling, and special services. Its congregation is made up of people in the greater Kansas City area, as well as retreatants, students, and others who are visiting the grounds.

USRS is dedicated to developing leadership within the Unity movement through both CEP and MEP. Between them, these two programs educate people who are interested in becoming licensed Unity teachers or ordained Unity ministers.

For the individual who wants to study for his or her own personal growth and unfoldment, there are two-week classes offered through CEP and week-long programs given by the Retreat Department.

The Library, Bookstore, and Counseling and Resource Center offer invaluable assistance to the other USRS departments. The Unity Library is one of the largest metaphysical libraries in the world, containing over 40,000 volumes. The Bookstore sells classroom textbooks for the Ministerial and Continuing Education programs. The Counseling Center is available for the students, retreatants, and the many visitors who come to the Village each year.

While addressing the question of spiritual education, Charles and Myrtle have said, "The doors of Unity swing in for all who want to come and study, and they swing out just as readily for those who want to go forth and teach" (*The Story of Unity*, p. 185). Through Unity School for Religious Studies, Unity School of Christianity has committed itself to keeping those doors swinging in both directions, meeting the spiritual education needs of people around the world.

Robert R. Barth

Library staff oversees a collection of more than 40,000 volumes.

The Continuing Education Program

ity students attending the 1928 Unity Convention at
nsas City, Missouri

As a major function of the education ministry, CEP provides educational opportunities for persons in all walks of life who are seeking practical principles for living more joyously and successfully.

Most CEP students attend classes to attain greater personal unfoldment. Some study to meet the requirements for licensed teacher recognition by the Association of Unity Churches. Still others endeavor to fulfill the requirements for application to the USRS Ministerial Education Program.

The Programs

Educational programs include resident studies that draw hundreds of persons to Unity Village in six two-week sessions a year. Extension study courses are also available in many local Unity ministries, taught by qualified Unity ministers and teachers.

Resident Study

The resident study program is structured into six sessions, each of two weeks' duration. Students may attend as many of these sessions as they wish and may earn up to 25 credits in one session. Each session offers basic and advanced courses.

Extension Study

The extension study program is an educational activity conducted jointly by USRS and the Association of Unity Churches. It provides for certain CEP classes to be taught in Unity ministries by accredited licensed teachers and licensed or ordained Unity ministers. The credit earned in these classes applies toward fulfillment of requirements for graduation from CEP.

The Ministerial Education Program

The work of the Unity movement includes many areas requiring effective ministerial leadership. The Ministerial Education Program (MEP) is preparation for ministerial leadership. Ministerial leadership in Unity is found in ministries of the Association of Unity Churches, chaplaincy positions in the military and in institutions, and in certain administrative positions in the Association and at Unity School.

Graduation ceremony

1988 Ministerial Education Program graduat

Unity teachers graduating class of 1934

History

The Ministerial Education Program was established by USRS in 1983, entering its first-year class in July of that year. Its development follows a long history of ministerial education, beginning with the Unity Training School in the 1930s. In 1945, a Ministerial Training Program was established in Silent Unity on a year-round basis. This was followed by the Unity Education Department in 1966. In 1969, the School for Ministerial and Religious Studies was developed by the Association of Unity Churches. Later, the name was changed to Unity Ministerial School.

The Ministerial Education Program is presently a two-year resident school structured in four ten-week quarters. Students admitted to the program undergo an intensive admissions process, including interviews and testing. Thirty-five to forty students are admitted each July. Graduation occurs in June of each year and graduates are eligible for recognition by the Association of Unity Churches as licensed Unity ministers.

The Unity Retreat staff (1988)

The Unity retreat program began in 1951, with the Unity Retreat for Prayer and Peace. Retreats have been conducted throughout the year on a regular basis at Unity Village since that time. Beginning in 1952, a schedule of four or five retreats a year was instituted. As the retreats became more popular, more were added to the schedule. Now twelve to thirteen retreats are held annually, with as many as 250 attending one retreat.

Retreats at Unity Village have been called "spiritual pep rallies." For many who attend, it is an adventure in spiritual growth. These are times of joy, fellowship, learning, and quiet meditation. The programs are presented in a way that is acceptable to persons of all religious backgrounds. Many of the retreatants are persons associated with religious organizations other than Unity.

The setting of Unity Village is conducive to a valid retreat experience. It is a place of natural beauty and inspiration. There are quiet glens and groves for personal reflection.

The programs are varied, and each retreatant is free to attend whatever meetings he or she desires. There are inspirational messages, times of guided meditation, workshops for delving more deeply into an understanding of the omnipresence of God, Bible lessons, and times of deep, joyous fellowship. Encouraging personal creativity, a talent show is held during each retreat. There are also recreational activities available. Swimming, golf, and tennis are popular with retreatants.

In the course of modern living, the demands on the average person are heavy. Often spiritual development is relegated to some secondary or tertiary place. Because of this, a time set aside for personal spiritual retreat is important.

Here are some comments received from retreatants:

"What a beautiful experience! My spirit was lifted and my consciousness expanded. Each time a negative thought, word, or action tried to creep in, I realized how inappropriate it was—simply out of context—and it vanished. I pray to retain this level of awareness on my return to the outside world. The visit to Silent Unity proved a rare treat and spiritual experience. Knowing that my letter to God and prayer requests will be remembered continuously in prayer brings hope and serenity each day."

***

"During my working years, when I would find myself under great stress I used to jokingly say, 'Stop, world, and let me off.' I never realized there was actually a place where you could get off—and then get back on—like a Unity retreat."

***

Retreatants sharing a silent meditation

"The retreat will remain in my heart as a very special spiritual experience: God's gift to me of love, friendship, inner awareness, and newfound enlightenment. My life has been blessed and I can feel God at work in it with me. Each day is rich with new insights, new lessons to learn, new ways of seeing God and thanking God. I know I am on the right path."

In a real sense, retreats only begin at the Village. Seeds are planted that must germinate and flourish when the retreatants return to their homes. It will not be back to what had been considered "normal" living. It will be different, because the person will be changed.

Activities Center at night during the Christmas season

People of Like Minds Gather

Glenn Mosley
Executive Director
Association of Unity Churches

As people develop interest in the Unity teachings and way of life, they naturally gravitate to others who share their ideas. From such gatherings of like-minded individuals, Unity churches (or centers) are formed.

These gatherings attain varying degrees of formality, depending upon the needs and desires of the people involved. Three stages commonly recognized by those involved in Unity are informal prayer groups, study groups, and churches. To provide networking opportunities and many other services, the Association of Unity Churches (Association) was formed.

The Association is a service organization of approximately 525 Unity churches and hundreds of study groups and informal prayer groups throughout the world.

A Unity church is incorporated as a not-for-profit organization and operates with bylaws approved by the membership. The governing body is the board of directors from within the membership and the minister working as a team. The minister is the administrative director and chief executive officer.

What Is a Unity Minister

Jim Rosemergy
Minister, Unity on the Plaza
Kansas City, Missouri

Since there have been ministers, people have looked to them for help in meeting the challenges of life and in discovering the reason for being. Unity ministers respond to human hurt and the search for meaning in ways transcending the human condition and its trials and tribulations. Yet, if you asked 100 of these servants of God and humankind, "What is a Unity minister?" they would reply in 100 different ways.

However, there would be a common thread. "Awake, O sleeper . . . and Christ shall give you light" (Eph. 5:14) conveys the purpose and the message of a Unity minister. His or her individual purpose is to awaken spiritually, and then to be a gentle hand on the shoulder that quickens in others the desire to become conscious of what it is to be beloved of God.

The Kingdom of Heaven Is at Hand

Jesus began His ministry with this powerful realization, ". . . the kingdom of heaven is at hand" (Mt. 4:17). This was the central message of Jesus' life, and it is the heart of the Unity work. Not only is heaven at hand or within our grasp, but it is as Jesus declared, "in the midst of you" (Lk. 17:21).

Some believe Spirit is separate from creation, and therefore towers of Babel are built in an attempt to reach God. Unity ministers do not support the building of the tower. They cry out to the people, "God is closer than hands and feet and breathing."

Charles Fillmore, co-founder of Unity, once said that the most important verse in the Bible is, " . . . Christ in you, the hope of glory" (Col. 1:27). Paul, in writing these words to the Colossians, referred to this revelation as a *mystery*, hidden for ages and generations. Paul encountered Jesus on the road to Damascus and awoke from his hate and human slumber, and in his wakefulness he discovered the Christ within him.

For Paul and a Unity minister, the Christ is the spiritual essence of every man, woman, and child. The Christ is the mysterious image of God within each of us, waiting in silent repose to be made manifest.

The reflecting pool

The fountain in the Rose Garden

Paul's insight is the foundation of the Unity contention that our *nature* is not sinful. Our nature, our ground of being, is the image of God, therefore divine. Acknowledging that human actions often affirm that we have forgotten this great truth, it is also evident that the mystery needs to be made manifest. A Unity minister aspires to let the Christ live as him or her and to quicken in others this same life by treating them as the sons or daughters of God they truly are.

Every minister believes in the power of prayer, and many call upon prayer to change the world. But a Unity minister believes that when one is in prayer, there is nothing to change. All ministers strive to correct the woes and ills of the world, but a Unity minister first corrects his or her *vision* of the world.

Prayer is practiced from the understanding that indecision, sickness, lack, and anxiety exist in human consciousness but are not present when one rests consciously in the Presence. Therefore, the purpose of prayer is not to change these conditions but to awaken to a consciousness of God where these conditions have no power.

For a Unity minister, God is the only presence and the only power. God is enough. Prayer is not something done solely during times of trouble and turmoil. Prayer is the life to live. It is not enough that only the minister is prayerful. A Unity minister knows that all people are destined to live a life of prayer.

Overseas Activities

Unity lake

The message of Unity eventually found its way across the seas to many countries of the world. It traveled mainly on the wings of *Daily Word*. This little book, with its message of Truth, has touched the hearts and minds of people everywhere, and people in foreign countries often found themselves devoted to the little magazine without realizing there was an organization called Unity, or even a place called Unity School. To many of them it did not matter, *Daily Word* was enough for them. But others felt the need to learn more about Truth and the Unity movement that was behind the publishing of *Daily Word*, and they made personal contact with headquarters.

In many places, with the exception of the USSR, Asia, and a few other countries, there are now established Unity study groups, churches, and centers. But the vast majority of Unity followers overseas are still individuals who start their day with *Daily Word*.

To people overseas, as is the case with so many people in the United States, Unity is primarily a healing prayer ministry. Because the need for physical healing is, perhaps, humanity's greatest single need, this one aspect of the ministry has appealed to most people who look to Unity for inspiration.

Serving Behind the Scenes

An organization as large and complex as Unity School of Christianity requires hundreds of people and services "behind the scenes," keeping things running smoothly, maintaining order and cleanliness, keeping records, supplying machinery, knowledge, and people.

In the following pages you will learn of some of these people and services. But one book cannot possibly tell the story of the entire network of important services involved in the Unity work. Along with those already mentioned, and those you will read about in the ensuing pages, there are people at Unity whose ministries are vital to the prayer work, the publications, the training of teachers and ministers. There are people in legal services, who see to it that copyright and other laws are met. And the accounting and treasury services are an important function in the judicious use of the funds so generously donated to the Unity work. These people must keep track of every penny earned and spent so that the publishing, prayer, and educational ministries can continue to operate efficiently.

With hundreds of thousands of books, magazines, other literature, audio-cassettes and videocassettes on hand for mailing to those who want them, a vast inventory record-keeping system is necessary.

All these and many other services receive little public attention but are vital in the continuing ministry of Unity. The efforts and dedication of the people performing these important tasks cannot be overestimated, for without them, the efficiency and quality of all the work would be seriously diminished.

Unity Inn

Unity founders, Charles and Myrtle Fillmore, chose to follow a vegetarian diet. Records indicate that Myrtle received instruction in vegetarianism in 1895 from Harry Church, who had recently adopted the Unity philosophy. Myrtle changed to a vegetarian diet at that time, and Charles soon followed.

In the beginning, meals at Unity were offered only to workers and were served in a common meal fashion. In 1906 the food service facility occupied the ground floor of Unity headquarters at Ninth and Tracy in Kansas City and service was expanded to include the general public. The net income for the first month was recorded at $84.72. Food was not priced; meals were offered on a freewill offering basis.

Interior decor and Dedicated workers, of Unity Inn, Ninth and Tracy, Kansas City, Missouri (circa 1925)

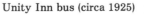

Unity Inn bus (circa 1925)

erior of early Unity Inn at the Village (circa 1960)

Word of the fine vegetarian bill of fare spread and the Unity cafeteria grew in popularity. In 1920 a building was erected on the corner of the Unity property at Ninth and Tracy to house the facility. The cafeteria's reputation soon became known nationwide. It was not uncommon to find visitors from many states sharing food and fellowship at the downtown location, and this is true today at the present location.

Although the Fillmores followed a strict vegetarian diet themselves and encouraged others in this practice, they did not make it a requirement for Unity followers. Their belief that each person must be free to follow his or her own inner guidance precluded this kind of approach.

Today, the Unity Inn offers a full menu including meat entrees. The Inn staff strives to provide the best food possible and to meet the various dietary needs of Unity workers and friends. Menus include fresh vegetables and fruits in season, sugarless desserts and other dishes, a vegetarian entree at each meal, and fresh salads and breads. The staff also obtains and prepares food to meet special dietary needs upon request.

The Unity Inn serves the needs of Unity workers and friends in a practical way . . . a way that feeds both body and soul. Good food, smiling faces, and an environment that says, "We're glad you're here," make sharing a meal at the Inn an experience to remember.

Charles and Myrtle Fillmore with friends (circa 1900)

Dedicated Unity employees (circa 1930)

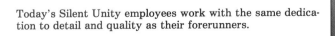

Today's Silent Unity employees work with the same dedication to detail and quality as their forerunners.

Unity bindery workers (circa 1912)

In 1889, the task of getting the message of Truth to the world fell to two people, Charles and Myrtle Fillmore. As committed as they were to sharing these ideas, it was not an easy undertaking. In the December 1889 issue of *Modern Thought*, Charles Fillmore wrote:

"We beg the pardon of our contributors and readers for the typographical and other errors that appear in these pages. Could they understand that everything but the typesetting is done by one man, and that that one man also labors in another field for the support of himself and family, they would certainly judge leniently. Our correspondents should also be charitable and not expect prompt responses to their letters—in fact they should consider themselves fortunate if they get any response whatever."

Times have changed and the Unity family has grown. Today, more than 600 full-time employees and an additional 100 seasonal employees work together to fulfill the commitment to spreading the message of Truth. " . . . All the activities of Unity School are designed to help people understand their own spiritual nature and to express spirituality in their lives in practical ways . . . " (Unity School's Statement of Purpose, 1987).

Form letters were printed on this writer press in 1916.

The Personnel Department serves in a support capacity for all departments and employees of Unity School. This ministry of service begins with an awareness that God is in charge, and with an understanding that there is a right place for each person.

A trained personnel staff provides recruiting services, screening, testing, and initial interviewing for Unity School departments. The interviewer identifies the skill requirements for each position and matches the individual's skills with the position so that the needs of the individual and the needs of the organization are met.

Identifying and responding to the needs of those who serve here is an important consideration for the School. The personnel staff also recommends and administers programs designed to assist Unity School employees in all aspects of their lives. Services available to employees include career counseling, family and personal counseling, discounts on meals and Unity materials, education assistance, health and recreation programs, a community garden, and retirement counseling.

Today, as in 1889, people throughout the world are helped because of the dedication and commitment of those who serve here. Unity workers, like workers everywhere, come from a variety of religious backgrounds. Whatever the religious preference, there is a common bond among Unity workers—a sense of satisfaction in knowing that they are contributing to something that makes a difference in people's lives. One knows, also, that a commitment to helping others was a part of the consciousness of all those who have gone before—those who have shared in this work for the past 100 years.

Unity employees enjoyed walking on the grounds and watching the construction progress at the new Silent Unity building.

A beautiful display was prepared for the 1988 Unity Conference as an invitation to visit Unity Village for the centennial celebration in 1989.

Public Relations

The Public Relations Department was established in 1975 to provide a central source of information about programs and activities conducted at Unity Village and to respond to inquiries about the work of Unity School and the Unity movement.

The School's approach to public relations follows the same low-key tradition established by Unity co-founders Charles and Myrtle Fillmore. The Fillmores saw themselves as teachers. They did not go about trying to win converts, and they said over and over that they were not trying to establish a new church or sect. Their mission was to share ideas that would help people understand their own spiritual potential and improve the quality of life.

People came to the Fillmores for prayer and instruction. They held meetings to share their ideas; however, students were always encouraged to think for themselves and to discover the Truth within. Unity School of Christianity was founded as a scientific, educational institution (*The Story of Unity*). A hallmark of the organization was its spirit of joy and tolerance, even with those who disagree. The founders' belief that there is some Truth in all teachings and that individuals must be free to find it for themselves provided the foundation for the exploration of ideas and tolerance of all those who are seeking the Truth.

Although the Fillmores did not proselytize, they were good neighbors . . . active in the community and always ready to lend a helping hand. As a result of their lifestyle, many of their neighbors became staunch Unity supporters.

The same philosophical guidelines of responding rather than promoting are followed today. The Public Relations staff of dedicated Unity people serve as goodwill ambassadors to workers, visitors, and the community. The department works with the local news media to assure correct information is available to the public. Staff members also represent the School in the community as speakers and as members of civic and service organizations.

Free guided tours of the School are provided for more than 3,500 visitors each year through this ministry of service. An audiovisual tour is available for those individuals who do not wish to take the hour-and-a-half walking tour.

The Public Relations Department, located in the Visitors Center, maintains a full-service post office for workers and visitors. The post office processes more than 86,000 pieces of mail each year.

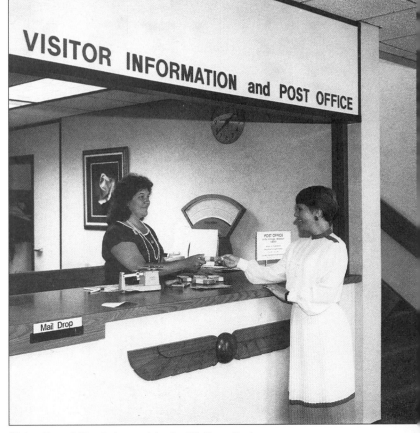

Unity Post Office is located in the Visitors Center.

"The divine ideas of faith, love, and joy have always permeated the daily activities of Unity School."

An alert staff keeps workers informed of happenings at the School through the organizational newsletter, *Unity Village News*. The purpose of the newsletter, first published in January 1916, is the same today, " . . . to promote in a general way the spirit of Unity among its workers; to further an acquaintance and understanding between workers and departments; and to foster a genial, kindly feeling and a spirit of good fellowship generally."

The Public Relations staff also maintains Unity's radio and TV outreach and coordinates the activities of the School's Speakers Bureau for Unity School folks who are invited to speak in the field.

Through all of its services, the aim of the Public Relations Department is to help present an accurate picture of Unity through information and a gentle presence that shows what Unity is all about.

The Rose Garden

Inside maintenance employees install new electrical wiring.

Unity Village . . . a breath of the Mediterranean in the Midwest. The buildings at Unity range in age from the homes of Rick and Lowell Fillmore, Myrtle's "The Arches," and the Pool Clubhouse, all built in the 1920s, to the beautiful new Silent Unity building just completed. The blend of Cotswold architecture for the older homes and the Mediterranean style of the main buildings with the beautiful fountains and Rose Garden form a unique whole that must be seen to be fully appreciated.

The spacious grounds (about 1,600 acres) are home to about 220 workers and resident students as well as many animals. From the beginning Unity grounds have been considered a sanctuary for wildlife. Flocks of Canada geese winter on the lakes and raise their young before returning to their northern homes. Wild turkey, deer, and small animals are plentiful. The only hunting permitted is with camera, sketch pad, or binoculars.

The grounds and buildings require constant, careful planning and maintenance.

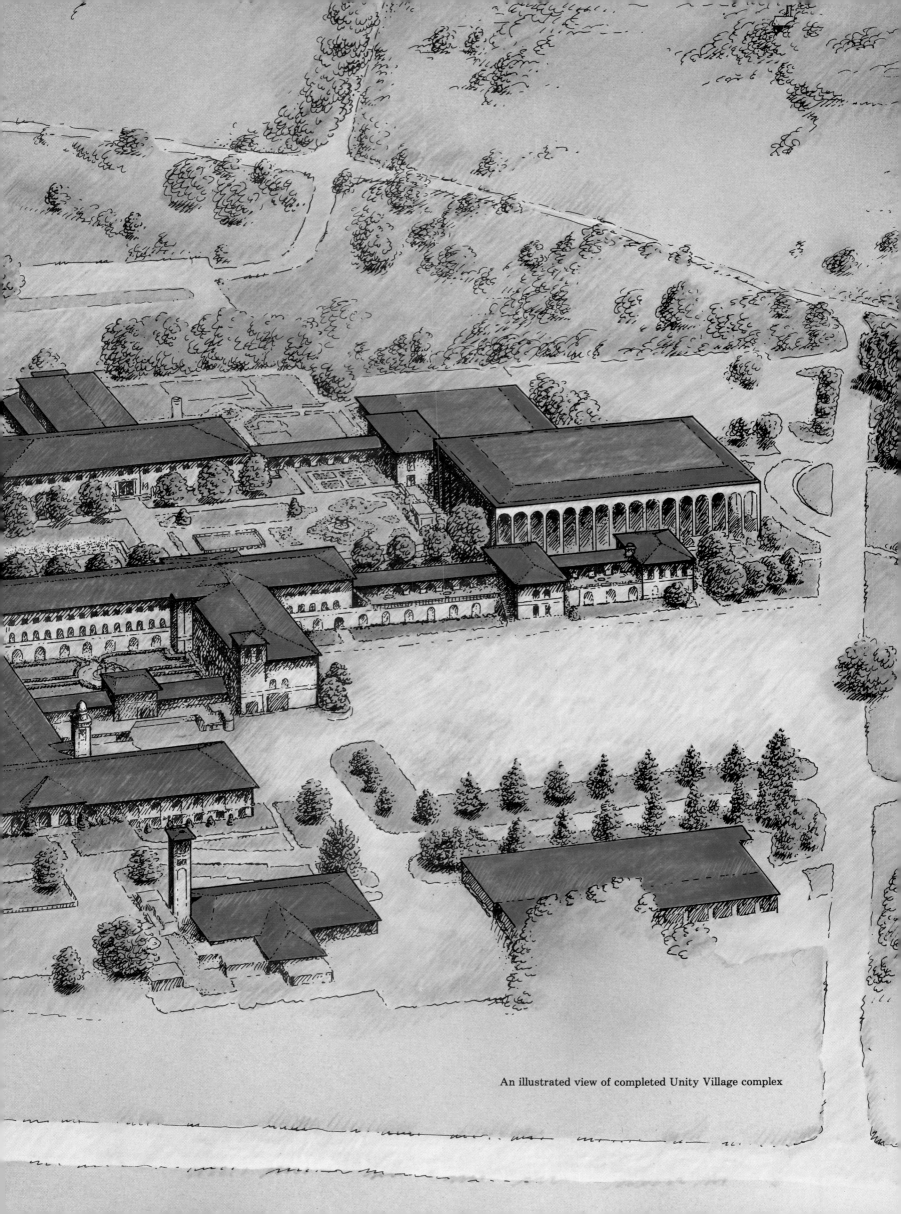

An illustrated view of completed Unity Village complex

Ducks and Canada geese on one of the two lakes at Unity Village

New Horizons for Unity and You

Eric Butterworth
Minister, Unity Center
of Practical Christianity
New York, New York

"Quo Vadis?" asked the Romans of old. As we join in the centennial celebration of Unity's origin, all of us who are interested in the Unity movement—teachers, ministers, students—should be asking ourselves the same question: Where are we going? If we were possessed of prophetic vision, we might look ahead to the year 2089 (100 years from now). Can you imagine where the Unity movement will be?

I have been involved personally in various aspects of this movement for more than 60 years. I have seen great changes, and I have observed the development of definite trends. I have an idealistic vision of what Unity is and should become, so some of the trends have been exciting to witness. However, some trends have been a matter of concern.

Much of my work as a spokesman for Unity has been through the medium of radio broadcasting, where for more than 40 years I have reached out and touched people in most of the major cities of America. There are people of all religious involvements and those who have none,

Lowell Fillmore Garden

important, the achievement of a great church with vast congregations and towering church edifices, or a long continuity of lives helped, and healed, even saved, and a widespread perception of Unity as an altruistic teaching that millions of people employ in their everyday lives?

It is my strong feeling that it would be a mistake for Unity to become another church (albeit a finer one), dispensing its theology of custom-made convictions (albeit metaphysical ones). It would be a pity if this great movement, the lengthened shadow of Charles and Myrtle Fillmore, were to slip into what Emerson calls "the sectarian rut." Yet how subtly does the system evolve of taking "Lessons in Truth," passing the course, becoming a member of the church (or center), and then settling into the age-old pattern that Bliss Carman so classically sings about: "They're praising God on Sunday, they'll be all right on Monday . . . it's just a little habit they've acquired."

Winter scene of Amphitheater gate

This is the important role of love, the language of Spirit, the key to the unspoken word of Truth. More than anything else Unity School and Unity centers and churches will become laboratories for the study and practice of the reality of creative love. We will realize and spread the word to communities everywhere with the same sort of seriousness with which we deal with nuclear fission, that the absence of love between persons or nations can destroy the world. Thus we will work to condition people to a universal law of love, much in the way we are taught to obey the civil law. This law will articulate the principle that maintaining the flow of mutuality and love is everybody's business. This was the lofty vision of Teilhard de Chardin, "Someday, after mastering the winds, the waves, and gravity, we will harness the energies of love. And then, for the second time in the history of the world, man will discover fire."

Number one fairway and Clubhouse at Unity Village Golf Course

To carry out its great mission in the age to come, Unity will need to take a careful inventory of the attitudes of the teacher and the teaching. It is probably true that every person is looking for someone who will tell him how to change his life, and subconsciously he looks for someone who will do it for him. The teacher must resist the ego-temptation to be that one. Gibran says, "No man can reveal to you aught, but that which already lies half asleep in the dawning of your knowledge . . . If the teacher is wise he does not bid you enter the house of *his* wisdom, but rather leads you to the threshold of your own mind."

Much as he may want to do so, the teacher cannot change you. That can only come from within yourself. The answers to your problems, and the power and potential for achieving them, are in you. No one can give them to you. Truth deals with spiritual development, but remember the word *develop* is the opposite of *envelop*, thus it means "to unfold from within."

144

Unity Tower in the fall

practice of healing. But if Unity is to reach the heights of its potential, and even to fulfill the goals of Charles Fillmore, it must seek and maintain a loftier perspective. As long as Unity, either in the ministry of Silent Unity or of the Unity centers and churches in the field, comes to be known as the place where you go to learn how to make "miracle demonstrations," it will never reach its potential as the great world movement it can be.

In an editorial in the June 1894 issue of *Unity* magazine, Charles Fillmore set down this challenge for Unity early along in its development. He said, "To maintain the religious dignity of the doctrine we advocate, we must hold to the pivotal thought that it is a spiritual ministry, and not a new system of healing. The healing that follows an understanding of the doctrine is not good in itself, and should not be proclaimed as good—it is the effect of the good."

If Unity can give emphasis to this ideal of the spiritual ministry, it may be perceived, not as just another system of practical metaphysics—one among many—but a very special movement of Christian mysticism. If Unity is able to imbue people who come to it for aid with loftier spiritual goals than the mere eradication of disease and poverty, and to inspire them to reach for a more cosmic awareness of life, thus to become a vital part of the solution of the human problems in the world, it may yet go down in history as a great religious movement, and an authentic and authoritative source of a fine and ideal mysticism. It will require a lot of self-criticism, self-honesty, and a new wave of integrity. The question is, are we willing?

Unity: *A Haven of Truth*

Statement of *Purpose*

Connie Fillmore
President
Unity School of Christianity

"Unity School of Christianity is dedicated to teaching and demonstrating the spiritual Truth of life as taught by Jesus Christ. Unity believes that God is absolute good, everywhere present, within all persons, and is readily accessible to everyone.

"All the activities of Unity School are designed to help people understand their own spiritual nature and to express spirituality in their lives in practical ways. The outreaches and services of Unity School are evaluated on the basis of how well they meet the spiritual needs of people.

"Unity is committed to doing its part to bring forth God's divine plan for good and to spreading Truth throughout the world."

More than 100 years ago, Unity had its inception in the mind of Myrtle Fillmore. At that time, Myrtle did not consciously set out to develop a philosophy or found a movement. Her need was personal: healing. Her need was met, and out of that one event grew the work that spans the globe today.

Unity has never shifted its focus from meeting the personal needs of individuals. We are as committed today to bringing forth light, wholeness, and abundance as Myrtle was. We are a movement of practical Christianity, specializing in positive attitudes and optimism. The world needed what we had to say 100 years ago, and it needs it no less today.

A Unity Chronology

The young Charles Fillmore (circa 1869)

1845 Mary Caroline Page (Fillmore) was born in Pagetown, Ohio, August 6. As a small girl she adopted the name Myrtle. She was graduated from Oberlin College and later secured a teaching position in Clinton, Missouri. Not a robust person, she was reared in the belief that she was a semi-invalid and had inherited tuberculosis.

1854 Charles Sherlock Fillmore was born in St. Cloud, Minnesota, August 22.

1864 Charles was in a skating accident; his hip was dislocated, and disease of the hip developed, leaving him with a withered leg.

1869 Charles went to work as a printer's helper. He was tutored by Mrs. Edgar Taylor and was influenced by the writings of Shakespeare, Tennyson, Emerson, and Lowell. He later worked as a grocery clerk and in a bank.

1874 Charles left Minnesota for Caddo, just north of the Texas border in the Indian Territory that is now Oklahoma. Later that year he left Caddo for Denison, Texas.

1876 Charles met Myrtle Page in Texas.

1879 Charles became a mule-team driver in Colorado; he later became an assayer and sold real estate. Myrtle left Texas and returned to Clinton.

1881 Charles and Myrtle Fillmore married and settled in Colorado.

1882 Lowell Fillmore was born in Pueblo, Colorado.

Board of Trustees

Unity School of Christianity
Board of Trustees

Additional photo credits: Warner Dixon and Walt Mathison

Printed U.S.A.

Unity School of Christianity
Unity Village, MO 64065

001-0270-20M-9-88

NOTES & MEMORIES

NOTES & MEMORIES

NOTES & MEMORIES

NOTES & MEMORIES

NOTES & MEMORIES